# My Book About

# Joe. Biden

Tuscawilla Creative Services
CreateTeachInspire.com

For bulk orders, contact info@contacttcs.com.

All photographs in this book are in the public domain and were obtained from WhiteHouse.gov, the Library of Congress, or other government sources.

This publication is a work of humor. It is intended for entertainment purposes only.

ISBN: 978-1-941826-38-6

# How to Use this Book

Do you have something to say about Joe Biden?

Here's an opportunity to write your book about America's 46th President.

This book includes a mix of lined and blank pages so you can write or draw. It's also illustrated with photos you can write captions for or just use for inspiration.

Not sure what to write? Check the next page for a list of ideas.

Fill in your name on the title page, add a dedication, then turn to page 13 and begin writing.

You can fill in the table of contents as you go or when you've finished.

Finally, if you would prefer that no one else sees these instructions, carefully remove this page from the book. We recommend using an exacto knife.

Now you're ready to proudly display *My Book About Joe Biden*.

# Need some ideas to help you get started?
# Write your thoughts on:

- Your reaction when Joe Biden was elected.

- Joe Biden, the person—husband, father, grandfather.

- Joe Biden, the politician—how he has evolved during his years in the Senate, as Vice President, and as President.

- His impact on race relations.

- His impact on the standing of the United States in the world.

- The 2020 Democratic primaries.

- The 2020 general election.

- Issues related to the legitimacy of the 2020 election.

- Joe Biden's immigration policies.

- His economic policies.

- His impact on U. S. relations with China.

- His reputation for verbal gaffs.

- His energy policies.

- His response to the pandemic.

- The legislation he was responsible for passing during his political career.

- His record as a Senator.

- His record as Vice President.

- The executive orders he signed after he was inaugurated.

# My Book About

# Joe Biden

## By

_____

*Dedication*

_____

_____

_____

_____

_____

_____

_____

_____

_____

_____

# Contents

_____

_____

_____

_____

_____

_____

_____

_____

_____

_____

_____

_____

_____

_____

_____

_____

_____

_____

_____

_____

_____

_____

_____

_____

_____

_____

_____

_____

_____

_____

_____

_____

_____

_____

_____

_____

_____

_____

_____

_____

_____

_____

_____

_____

_____

_____

_____

_____

_____

_____

_____

_____

_____

_____

_____

_____

_____

_____

_____

_____

_____

_____

_____

_____

_____

_____

_____

_____

_____

_____

_____

_____

_____

_____

_____

_____

_____

_____

_____

_____

_____

_____
_____
_____
_____
_____
_____
_____
_____
_____
_____
_____
_____
_____
_____
_____
_____
_____

_____

_____

_____

_____

_____

_____

_____

_____

_____

_____

_____

_____

_____

_____

_____

_____

_____

_____

_____

_____

_____

_____

_____

_____

_____

_____

_____

_____

_____

_____

_____

_____

_____

_____

_____

_____

_____

_____

_____

_____

_____

_____

_____

_____

_____

_____

_____

_____

_____

_____

_____

_____

_____

_____

_____

_____

_____

_____

_____

_____

_____

_____

_____

_____

_____

_____

_____

_____

_____

_____

_____

_____

_____

_____

_____

_____

_____

_____

_____

_____

_____

_____

_____

_____

_____

_____

_____

_____

_____

_____

_____

_____

_____

_____

_____

_____

_____

_____

_____

_____

_____

_____

_____

_____

_____

_____

_____

_____

_____

_____

_____

_____

_____

_____

_____

_____

_____

_____

_____

_____

_____

_____

_____

_____

_____

_____

_____

_____

_____

_____

_____

_____

_____

_____

_____

_____

_____

_____

_____

_____

_____

_____

_____

_____

_____

_____

_____

_____

_____

_____

_____

_____

_____

_____

_____

_____

_____

_____

_____

_____

_____

_____

_____

_____

_____

_____

_____

_____

_____

_____

_____

_____

_____

_____

_____

_____

_____

_____

_____

_____
_____
_____
_____
_____
_____
_____
_____
_____
_____
_____
_____
_____
_____
_____
_____
_____
_____
_____
_____

_____

_____

_____

_____

_____

_____

_____

_____

_____

_____

_____

_____

_____

_____

_____

_____

_____

_____

_____

_____

_____

_____

_____

_____

_____

_____

_____

_____

_____

_____

_____

_____

_____

_____

_____

_____

_____

_____

_____

_____

_____

_____

_____

_____

_____

_____

_____

_____

_____

_____

_____

_____

_____

_____

_____

_____

_____

_____

_____

_____
_____
_____
_____
_____
_____
_____
_____
_____
_____
_____
_____
_____
_____
_____
_____
_____

160 | *My Book About*

# Other Titles in the
## *My Book About* Series

Get a complete list of available titles:

CreateTeachInspire.com/mybook

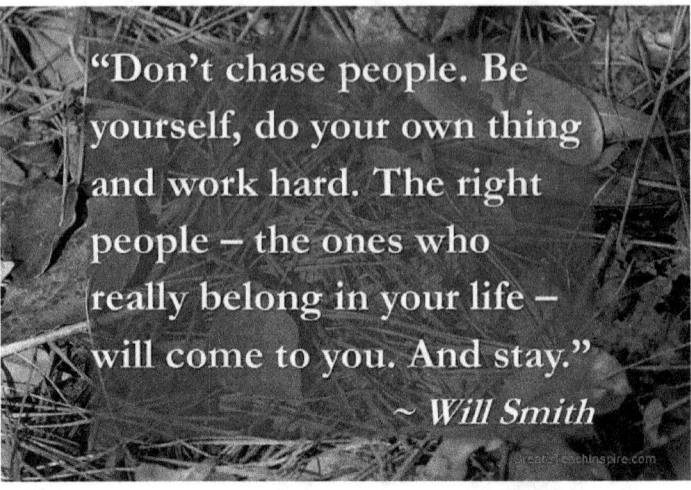

"Don't chase people. Be yourself, do your own thing and work hard. The right people – the ones who really belong in your life – will come to you. And stay."
~ *Will Smith*

"I often warn people: Somewhere along the way, someone is going to tell you, 'There is no "I" in team.' What you should tell them is, 'Maybe not. But there is an "I" in independence, individuality and integrity."
- *George Carlin*

"In a survey of 90-year-olds, when asked what they would have done differently, they responded, 'Risk more, reflect more and leave a legacy that matters.'"
- *Dr. Linda Livingstone*
*Dean of Pepperdine University Business School*

# 10 Seconds of Inspiration

Get images like these delivered to your inbox every Saturday morning. Enjoy and share!

Visit

## CreateTeachInspire.com/ss

### to join Shareable Saturday

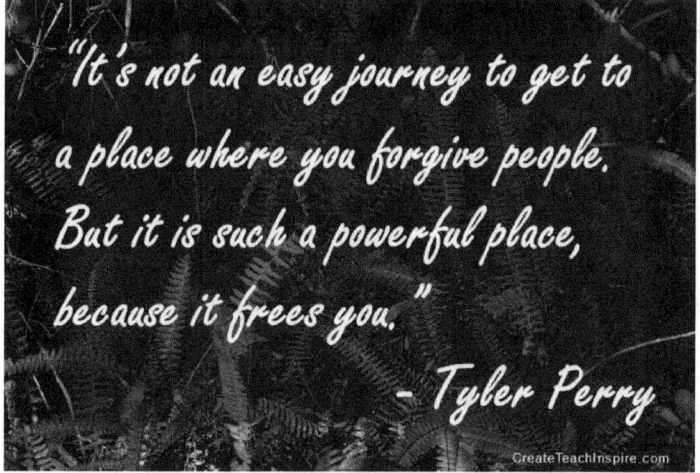

"You cannot get through a single day without having an impact on the world around you. What you do makes a difference, and you have to decide what kind of difference you want to make."

– Jane Goodall

CreateTeachInspire.com

"It's not an easy journey to get to a place where you forgive people. But it is such a powerful place, because it frees you."

– Tyler Perry

CreateTeachInspire.com

A great way to wrap up your week!

Visit **CreateTeachInspire.com/ss** to join Shareable Saturday